T0088416

Piano Sketches

Vitalij Neugasimov

Book 1

18 easy pieces for solo piano

MUSIC DEPARTMENT

OXFORD
UNIVERSITY PRESS

OXFORD
UNIVERSITY PRESS

Great Clarendon Street, Oxford OX2 6DP,
United Kingdom

Oxford University Press is a department of the University of Oxford.
It furthers the University's objective of excellence in research, scholarship,
and education by publishing worldwide. Oxford is a registered trade mark of
Oxford University Press in the UK and in certain other countries

This collection © Oxford University Press 2016

Vitalij Neugasimov has asserted his right under the Copyright, Designs
and Patents Act, 1988, to be identified as the Composer of these Works

Database right Oxford University Press (maker)

First published 2016

Impression: 6

All rights reserved. No part of this publication may be reproduced,
stored in a retrieval system, or transmitted, in any form or by any means,
without the prior permission in writing of Oxford University Press

Permission to perform this work in public (except in the course of divine worship) should normally be
obtained from the Performing Right Society Ltd (PRS) at www.prsformusic.com or
a local performing right licensing organization, unless the owner or the occupier
of the premises being used already holds a licence from such an organization.
Likewise, permission to make and exploit a recording must be obtained in advance from the
Mechanical-Copyright Protection Society Ltd (MCPS) at www.prsformusic.com or
a local mechanical copyright licensing organization

Enquiries concerning reproduction outside the scope of the above
should be directed to the Music Rights Department, Oxford University Press, at
music.permissions.uk@oup.com or at the address above

ISBN 978–0–19–341327–6

Music and text origination by Katie Johnston

Printed in Great Britain on acid-free paper by
Halstan & Co. Ltd, Amersham, Bucks.

Pieces from this collection originally published as part of
Pianoheads Collection 1 and *2* (2009 and 2010)

Contents

Frog Boogie	4
The Mouse and the Elephant	6
Lullaby	8
Blues for Lucy	9
Waltz-Caprice	10
Lazy Bear	12
Birthday March	13
Butterfly	14
Oriental Dance	16
Ballad for Robin Hood	17
Greetings from Cuba	18
Old Scottish Dance	20
Let's Rock	22
Moody Gigue	24
An Idyll	25
Toccata	26
Meditation	28
Walking Around	30

Composer's Note

Welcome to this short series of piano miniatures covering a broad spectrum of musical styles and gestures. Accessible yet engaging, the pieces should appeal melodically and harmonically to developing pianists, and provide opportunities for exploring musical textures and narrative while addressing technical points. They are written for player and listener alike, and hopefully inspire a sense of creativity and wonder at the palette of sound that is available to us.

This collection is dedicated to the memory of my beloved father, Vasilij Neugasimov. The pieces were inspired by my sister Liudmila Neugasimova, an outstanding piano teacher with over 20 years' experience; her encouragement and contribution were immense. I should like to thank, also, Martynas Vilkelis, who helped me to achieve my goal.

Frog Boogie

Vitalij Neugasimov

© Oxford University Press 2009 and 2016. Photocopying this copyright material is ILLEGAL.

17
sf
f
21
p
f
25
29
32
p

The Mouse and the Elephant

Vitalij Neugasimov

© Oxford University Press 2009 and 2016. Photocopying this copyright material is ILLEGAL.

11
mf
f
13
mf
15
f
17
p
19
f

Lullaby

Vitalij Neugasimov

© Oxford University Press 2010 and 2016. Photocopying this copyright material is ILLEGAL.

to my sister Liudmila

Blues for Lucy

Vitalij Neugasimov

Medium swing ♩ = 120 (♫ = ♩³♪)

© Oxford University Press 2009 and 2016. Photocopying this copyright material is ILLEGAL.

Waltz-Caprice

Vitalij Neugasimov

© Oxford University Press 2009 and 2016. Photocopying this copyright material is ILLEGAL.

21
f
25
29
mf
Fine
Trio
33
mf risoluto
f
38
poco rit.
a tempo
mp
43
rall.
D.C. al Fine

Lazy Bear

Vitalij Neugasimov

* Play the repeat on the D.C.

© Oxford University Press 2010 and 2016. Photocopying this copyright material is ILLEGAL.

Birthday March

Vitalij Neugasimov

© Oxford University Press 2010 and 2016. Photocopying this copyright material is ILLEGAL.

Butterfly

Vitalij Neugasimov

© Oxford University Press 2010 and 2016. Photocopying this copyright material is ILLEGAL.

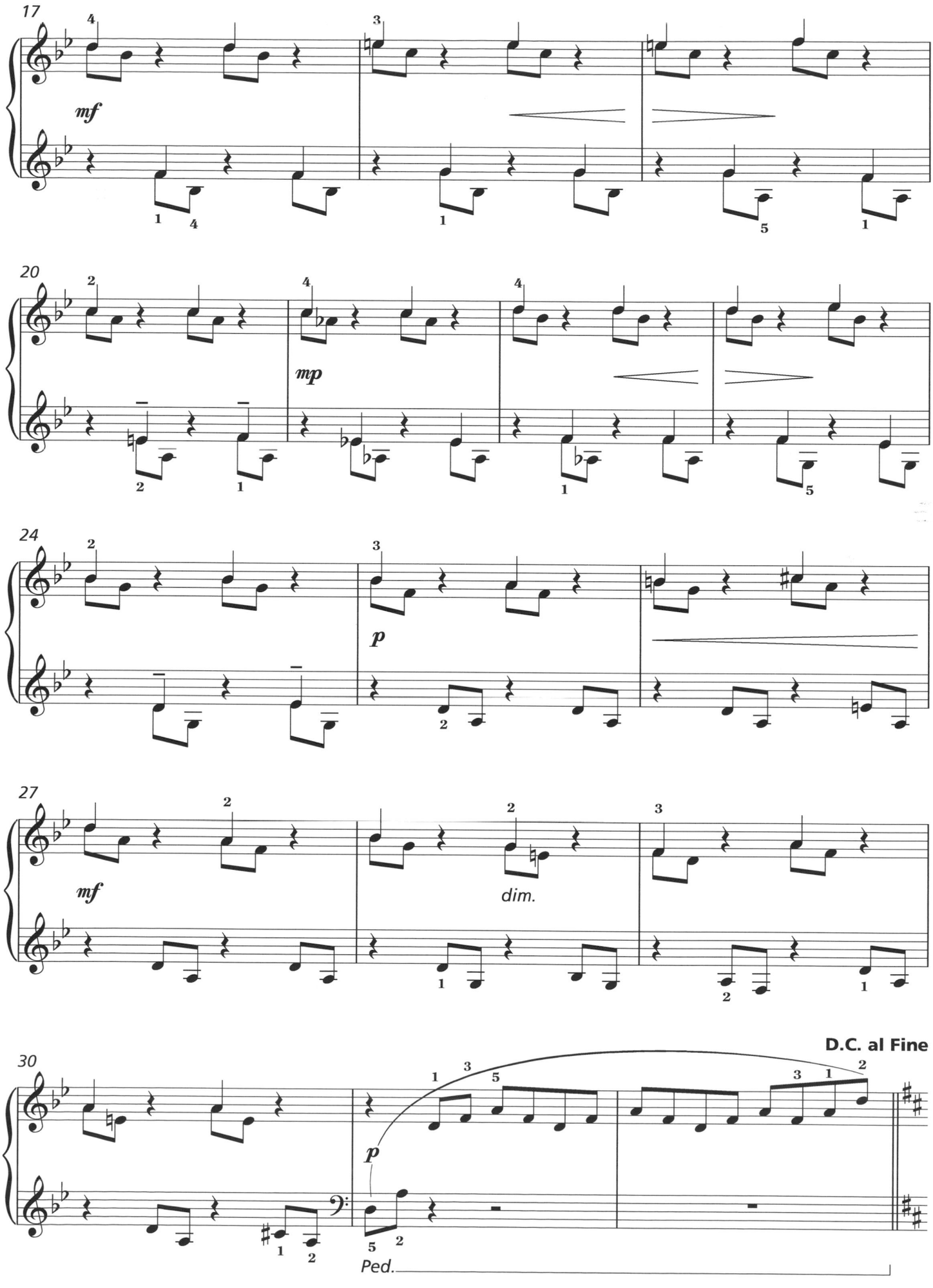
17
mf
20
mp
24
p
27
mf
dim.
30
p
D.C. al Fine
Ped.

Oriental Dance

Vitalij Neugasimov

* Play the repeat on the D.C.

© Oxford University Press 2009 and 2016. Photocopying this copyright material is ILLEGAL.

Ballad for Robin Hood

Vitalij Neugasimov

* All chords may be played *arpeggiato.*

© Oxford University Press 2009 and 2016. Photocopying this copyright material is ILLEGAL.

Greetings from Cuba

Vitalij Neugasimov

© Oxford University Press 2009 and 2016. Photocopying this copyright material is ILLEGAL.

21
p
25
5
cresc. poco a poco
29
5
f
1
ff marcato
mf
33
p
37
f

Old Scottish Dance

Vitalij Neugasimov

© Oxford University Press 2009 and 2016. Photocopying this copyright material is ILLEGAL.

17
p
mf
sim.
21
25
28
3
mp
poco rit.
31
a tempo
p
1
3
1
3
sf

Let's Rock

Vitalij Neugasimov

© Oxford University Press 2009 and 2016. Photocopying this copyright material is ILLEGAL.

13
mf
Ped.
Ped.
17
mp
p
Ped.
20
f
23
ff
poco rit.
26

Moody Gigue

Vitalij Neugasimov

© Oxford University Press 2009 and 2016. Photocopying this copyright material is ILLEGAL.

An Idyll

Vitalij Neugasimov

© Oxford University Press 2009 and 2016. Photocopying this copyright material is ILLEGAL.

Toccata

Vitalij Neugasimov

© Oxford University Press 2009 and 2016. Photocopying this copyright material is ILLEGAL.

11
Ped.
13
mf
sim.
15
17
p
19
f

Meditation

Vitalij Neugasimov

© Oxford University Press 2016. Photocopying this copyright material is ILLEGAL.

27
p
mf
32
37
dim.
41
pp
D.C. al Coda
poco rit.
47
CODA
49
rit.
dim.
pp

Walking Around

Vitalij Neugasimov

© Oxford University Press 2010 and 2016. Photocopying this copyright material is ILLEGAL.

17
mf
21
25